Rusty the Rascal

Wendy Graham
Illustrated by Margaret Power

Contents

Chapter 1
Poor Little Rusty

Andrea was the first one to hear the siren.

"What's going on?" she asked her brother, David.

The sound of the siren got louder and closer. David and Andrea ran to the window.

"It's an ambulance! And it's stopping next door at Mr. Tomkins' house," said David.

"I wonder what happened," said Andrea.

They hurried outside and watched as two paramedics carried Mr. Tomkins out of his house on a stretcher. Rusty, Mr. Tomkins' little dog, danced around their legs.

"What's wrong, Mr. Tomkins?" Andrea asked.

"It's my leg," Mr. Tomkins said. "I fell and I'm afraid it might be broken."

"You may have to stay in the hospital for a while," said the paramedic.

Mr. Tomkins' eyes dimmed. "Poor little Rusty. I have nobody to take care of him. I don't know what I'll do."

Andrea and David both had an idea.

"Mr. Tomkins," David said, "could we take care of Rusty for you?"

"I'm sure our parents wouldn't mind," said Andrea.

Mr. Tomkins smiled. "Oh, that would be good," he said. "I have to warn you, though, Rusty can be a rascal."

Luckily, Andrea and David's parents agreed that Rusty could stay. The children took Rusty into their backyard.

"He wants to play," said David. Rusty rolled over, paws in the air. David and Andrea laughed as Rusty fetched his ball and dropped it at their feet.

Andrea and David took turns shaking Rusty's outstretched paw.

That evening, Andrea took Rusty into the laundry room. "Now, Rusty," she said, "you can sleep in here. And in the morning we'll take you for a walk."

Rusty didn't understand, but when he heard his name he wagged his tail.

"Come on, Rusty," said Andrea as she patted his bed. "Lie down now."

Rusty was sleepy after the day's excitement so he lay down and went to sleep.

Chapter 2
The Escape

During the night, Rusty woke up and looked around. Moonlight was shining through the open laundry room window. He saw a tear in the screen! He jumped onto the dryer and wriggled his way out.

Rusty scampered happily down the street. He saw a mouse and chased it this way and that. Then the mouse disappeared into a storm-water drain near the curb. Rusty sniffed the drain and barked. Then nose first, he squeezed into the drain to find the mouse.

All of a sudden, Rusty was falling.
Down he fell into damp, smelly blackness.

He landed on a pile of wet leaves,
then Rusty got up and shook himself off.
Rusty looked for the mouse, but it had
already escaped down a small pipe.
He tried to jump out of the drain, but he
couldn't reach the opening. Rusty was
trapped in the storm-water drain!

The next morning when Andrea and David woke up, they went to the laundry room to see Rusty.

"Look! Rusty's gone!" David gasped.

"Oh, no!" Andrea said. "It's true, Rusty is a rascal! He must have escaped through the window. We have to find him!"

Andrea and David's parents helped look for him. They searched Mr. Tomkins' yard. They searched the nearby park. They searched the school playground. But they couldn't find Rusty anywhere!

Soon more people heard that Rusty was missing, and they helped look for him.

"Rusty!" they called, searching everywhere. "Rusty!"

The people at the corner store even put a sign in the window.

**Missing Dog
named Rusty**
• small
• rust-colored
• shaggy
If you find him
please call
555-9567

OPEN

A police car drove by and stopped. The police officer listened as Andrea and David told him what had happened to Rusty the Rascal.

"We're here to help," the police officer said. "We'll search for him, too." He put out a call over their radio so other police officers could join the search. "Please keep a lookout for a little dog with a rust-colored, shaggy coat."

Everyone tried hard to find him. But sadly, there was no sign of Rusty anywhere.

David and Andrea began walking home. "I'm worried," Andrea said. "We've looked everywhere! Where could he be?"

"Maybe he'll be waiting for us when we get home," said David. His stomach felt like it was all tied up in knots.

Chapter 3
Rescuing Rusty

Rusty had fallen asleep, but woke up when he heard familiar voices as the children walked by. He whimpered and scratched at the wall of the drain.

"David, I heard something," Andrea said.

Rusty whimpered a little louder.

"Where is it coming from?" asked David.

"Look!" said Andrea. "A little dog could easily fall down the storm-water drain."

David peered into the drain. "Rusty? Rusty, are you in there?"

When Rusty heard his name, he barked.

"It's him!" said Andrea. "I hope he's okay."

"It's a long way down," David said. "How will we get him out?"

"We could call the fire department,"
said a lady who had helped in the search.

"But what if the fire truck is needed for
a fire?" said Andrea.

"Let's call animal control," a neighbor
said. "That's a community service that helps
in animal emergencies like this."

Soon, an animal control van pulled up. The animal control worker got out and peered down the drain. "Okay, let's get you out of there," she said to Rusty.

First, she moved the heavy drain cover to the side. Rusty looked up at them and barked. Then she went to her van and got a long pole with a big net on one end. She lowered it down toward Rusty. She spoke to him in a kind voice. "It's okay, Rusty."

Gently, the worker scooped Rusty into the net and lifted him out of the drain.

Rusty was wet, cold, and smelly. But he was fine. He was so happy that his tail spun around like a helicopter propeller. He licked the animal control worker, as if to say *thank you*!

After Rusty's little adventure, David and Andrea made sure they closed the laundry room window at night.

David and Andrea took him for walks every day and took good care of him. But Rusty seemed different.

"Maybe he misses Mr. Tomkins," said Andrea.

"Probably," replied David. "They haven't been apart this long since Rusty was a puppy!"

That week, the local newspaper printed a story, along with a photo of the rescue. Soon everyone in town knew about Rusty's little adventure. Rusty loved the attention!

Chapter 4
A Good Idea

A few days later, Rusty was playing in the sunshine in Andrea and David's backyard.

"Rusty, Rusty!" a voice called out.

Rusty recognized the voice and wagged his tail with excitement.

"Hello, you rascal," said Mr. Tomkins, as he gave Rusty a pat. "I'm home!"

Andrea and David smiled as Rusty ran in circles and danced around on his hind legs.

"Well," Mr. Tomkins said, "it's good to see you haven't forgotten me."

Rusty rolled onto his back with his paws in the air.

Mr. Tomkins laughed. "Good dog! Now where's your ball, Rusty?" he said.

Rusty ran off and fetched his ball. He was very excited to see Mr. Tomkins again!

At school, Andrea and David told their friends that Mr. Tomkins was home from the hospital.

"We still take Rusty for walks, though," said David. "Mr. Tomkins can't walk far until his leg heals."

"I'm so glad Rusty's okay," said Milos. "I'd like a dog, but we aren't allowed to have one in our apartment."

"I can't have a dog either. My mom's allergic," said Kara. "If you ever need someone to walk Rusty, I'd like to help."

"Me, too," added Milos.

When Andrea and David walked Rusty that night, they saw Mrs. Holt from down the street.

"Hello," Mrs. Holt said. "I have a favor to ask. I am going out tomorrow night and

won't have time to walk our dog, Ralph.
Do you think you could walk him, too?"

"Sure," said David. "Actually, that gives
me an idea."

That night David and Andrea made a poster. "We can put the poster up at the store," said Andrea.

"Good idea, but let's show Mr. Tomkins first," said David.

The next day when they picked up Rusty for his walk, they showed Mr. Tomkins their poster.

"We are starting a dog walking service," said David. "And our friends from school will all be able to help out, too!"

"What a good idea," Mr. Tomkins said, admiring the poster. "You two are wonderful. The next time the town has an award for good citizens, I will vote for you both."

Andrea and David grinned.

"In a strange way," Mr. Tomkins said, "that fall has turned out to be a good thing."

"How?" asked Andrea.

"Well, people stop by now to see how I am, and to ask about Rusty," Mr. Tomkins said.

Rusty was chewing on an old bone, and wagged his tail when he heard his name.

Mr. Tomkins went on, "And the local government has arranged some services to help me. My meals are delivered every day, and a nurse comes regularly to check on my leg. So I have visitors that I never had before. But you two," he said, "are my favorite visitors of all."

Rusty wagged his tail as if he agreed. Then he dropped the bone into David's lap. It was smelly, and covered with dirt.

"Oh, dear. Rusty always brings things to people he likes," Mr. Tomkins laughed.

David picked up the bone. "Thank you, Rusty. It's just what we've always wanted." And everyone burst out laughing.

Living in a Community

Good Citizenship

Members of a community have rights and responsibilities. Good citizenship is one of the most important responsibilities. Good citizens respect others, and play fairly. They look for opportunities to help others, and do their part to make the community a safe and happy place to live.

Children help make a garden in a community playground.

Community Services

Animal Control

The government provides community services. Many communities have animal control services. These services deal with pets and wild animals. They make sure that people take care of their pets. They catch and take care of stray animals. Sometimes they rescue animals that need help or are in danger.

Animal control workers rescue a duck and take it to a safe place.

Think About the Story

In *Rusty the Rascal*, Andrea and David help their neighbor after he breaks his leg. Other people in the community help Mr. Tomkins and Rusty, too. Think about these questions.

- How do David and Andrea help Mr. Tomkins?
- How do people in the community help when Rusty goes missing?
- What service do Andrea and David start? How will it help their community?

To learn more about communities and living in the United States, read the books below.

SUGGESTED READING
Windows on Literacy
Serving the Community
Symbols of Freedom

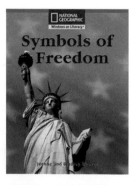